THE SALSA, DIP, SOUP, AND COLD SOUP COOKBOOK

50 DELICIOUS SALSA RECIPES, DIP RECIPES, SOUP, AND GAZPACHO RECIPES

By
BookSumo Press
Copyright © by Saxonberg Associates
All rights reserved

Published by
BookSumo Press, a DBA of Saxonberg Associates
http://www.booksumo.com/

ABOUT THE AUTHOR.

BookSumo Press is a publisher of unique, easy, and healthy cookbooks.

Our cookbooks span all topics and all subjects. If you want a deep dive into the possibilities of cooking with any type of ingredient. Then BookSumo Press is your go to place for robust yet simple and delicious cookbooks and recipes. Whether you are looking for great tasting pressure cooker recipes or authentic ethic and cultural food. BookSumo Press has a delicious and easy cookbook for you.

With simple ingredients, and even simpler step-by-step instructions BookSumo cookbooks get everyone in the kitchen chefing delicious meals.

BookSumo is an independent publisher of books operating in the beautiful Garden State (NJ) and our team of chefs and kitchen experts are here to teach, eat, and be merry!

INTRODUCTION

Welcome to *The Effortless Chef Series*! Thank you for taking the time to purchase this cookbook.

Come take a journey into the delights of easy cooking. The point of this cookbook and all BookSumo Press cookbooks is to exemplify the effortless nature of cooking simply.

In this book we focus on preparing Salsas, Dips, Soups, and Cold Soups. You will find that even though the recipes are simple, the taste of the dishes are quite amazing.

So will you take an adventure in simple cooking? If the answer is yes please consult the table of contents to find the dishes you are most interested in.

Once you are ready, jump right in and start cooking.

— BookSumo Press

TABLE OF CONTENTS

ANY ISSUES? CONTACT US

If you find that something important to you is missing from this book please contact us at info@booksumo.com.

We will take your concerns into consideration when the 2nd edition of this book is published. And we will keep you updated!

— BookSumo Press

LEGAL NOTES

COMMON ABBREVIATIONS

cup(s)	C.
tablespoon	tbsp
teaspoon	tsp
ounce	oz.
pound	lb

*All units used are standard American measurements

CHAPTER 1: EASY SALSA, DIP, SOUP, AND COLD SOUP RECIPES

HOMEMADE CHIPOTLE MAYONNAISE

Ingredients

- 1/2 C. mayonnaise
- 2 chipotle chilies in adobo sauce
- 1 tbsp adobo sauce from chipotle peppers

Directions

- Add all the ingredients in a food processor and pulse till well combined and smooth.

Amount per serving (8 total)

Timing Information:

Preparation	5 m
Cooking	5 m
Total Time	5 m

Nutritional Information:

Calories	101 kcal
Fat	11 g
Carbohydrates	0.8g
Protein	0.1 g
Cholesterol	5 mg
Sodium	103 mg

* Percent Daily Values are based on a 2,000 calorie diet.

CREAMY CHIPOTLE GUACAMOLE

Ingredients

- 2 avocados, peeled, seeded and cubed
- 1 tbsp fresh lime juice
- 2 tbsps sour cream
- 1/4 C. salsa, or to taste
- 1/4 tsp adobo sauce from canned chilies, or to taste
- salt and pepper to taste

Directions

- In a large bowl, all the ingredients except salt and black pepper.
- With a potato masher, mash till well combined and season with the salt and black pepper.

Amount per serving (8 total)

Timing Information:

Preparation	15 m
Cooking	15 m
Total Time	30 m

Nutritional Information:

Calories	91 kcal
Fat	8.1 g
Carbohydrates	5.1g
Protein	1.3 g
Cholesterol	2 mg
Sodium	55 mg

* Percent Daily Values are based on a 2,000 calorie diet.

CHIPOTLE YOGURT SAUCE

Ingredients

- 1/2 C. plain yogurt
- 1/2 C. mayonnaise
- 2 tsps pureed chipotle peppers in adobo sauce

Directions

- Add all the ingredients in a bowl and mix till well combined and smooth.
- Refrigerate to chill before serving.

Amount per serving (8 total)

Timing Information:

Preparation	2 m
Cooking	2 m
Total Time	4 m

Nutritional Information:

Calories	109 kcal
Fat	11.2 g
Carbohydrates	1.6g
Protein	0.9 g
Cholesterol	6 mg
Sodium	95 mg

* Percent Daily Values are based on a 2,000 calorie diet.

CHIPOTLE HUMMUS

Ingredients

- 2 (15.5 oz.) cans garbanzo beans, drained
- 1/2 C. water
- 1/4 C. tahini (sesame-seed paste)
- 1/4 C. fresh lemon juice
- 2 tbsps olive oil
- 1 canned chipotle pepper in adobo sauce
- 2 cloves garlic
- 1 1/2 tsps cumin
- 1 (7 oz.) jar roasted red bell peppers, drained
- 6 oil-packed sun-dried tomatoes, drained
- 1/2 C. chopped cilantro
- 1/2 tsp salt
- ground black pepper to taste

Directions

- In a food processor, add beans, tahini, chipotle pepper, garlic, oil and lemon juice and pulse till well combined and smooth.
- Add the remaining ingredients and pulse till chopped finely.

- Place the hummus in a bowl and refrigerate, covered before serving.

Amount per serving (20 total)

Timing Information:

Preparation	15 m
Cooking	15 m
Total Time	30 m

Nutritional Information:

Calories	90 kcal
Fat	3.7 g
Carbohydrates	11.9g
Protein	2.9 g
Cholesterol	0 mg
Sodium	235 mg

* Percent Daily Values are based on a 2,000 calorie diet.

CHIPOTLE TOMATO SALSA

Ingredients

- 1 (14.5 oz.) can whole peeled tomatoes
- 1 fresh jalapeno pepper, seeded
- 1 chipotle chili in adobo sauce, seeded
- 1 (1 inch) piece dried ancho chili pepper
- 1 clove garlic
- 2 1/2 tbsps chopped onion
- 1 tbsp chopped fresh cilantro
- 1 tbsp lemon juice, or to taste
- 3/4 tsp salt
- 1/4 tsp white sugar, or to taste
- 1/4 tsp ground cumin

Directions

- In a blender, add all the ingredients and pulse till desired consistency.
- Transfer into a bowl and keep aside till the flavors blend completely.

Amount per serving (8 total)

Timing Information:

Preparation	20 m
Cooking	1 h 20 m
Total Time	20 m

Nutritional Information:

Calories	14 kcal
Fat	0.2 g
Carbohydrates	3.2g
Protein	0.5 g
Cholesterol	0 mg
Sodium	299 mg

* Percent Daily Values are based on a 2,000 calorie diet.

CHIPOTLE CREAMY PUMPKIN SOUP

Ingredients

- 2 tbsps butter
- 2 tbsps all-purpose flour
- 4 C. vegetable stock
- 1 (29 oz.) can pumpkin puree
- 2 chipotle peppers in adobo sauce, minced
- 1 1/2 C. half-and-half cream
- 2 tbsps sofrito
- 1 tbsp Worcestershire sauce
- 1 tsp salt
- 1 tsp paprika

Directions

- In a large pan, melt the butter on medium heat and cook the flour stirring continuously for about 3 minutes or till it becomes golden brown.
- Slowly, add the broth, stirring continuously and bring to a boil on high heat.
- Slowly, add the pumpkin puree, stirring continuously and then stir in the half-and-half, Worcestershire sauce,

sofrito, chipotle peppers, salt and paprika and bring to a gentle simmer.

- Reduce the heat to medium-low and simmer, stirring occasionally for about 8 minutes or till thickens.

Amount per serving (8 total)

Timing Information:

Preparation	10 m
Cooking	20 m
Total Time	30 m

Nutritional Information:

Calories	145 kcal
Fat	9.5 g
Carbohydrates	13.3g
Protein	3.4 g
Cholesterol	24 mg
Sodium	790 mg

* Percent Daily Values are based on a 2,000 calorie diet.

Hot Chipotle Peach Salsa

Ingredients

- 1 C. sliced canned peaches, drained and chopped
- 1/3 C. chopped red onion
- 2 cloves garlic, minced
- 1 1/2 tsps minced fresh ginger root
- 2 tsps minced chipotle peppers in adobo sauce
- 1/3 C. chopped fresh cilantro
- 1/2 lime, juiced
- salt and pepper to taste

Directions

- In a large bowl, add all the ingredients and mix till well combined.
- Refrigerate to chill before serving.

Amount per serving (4 total)

Timing Information:

Preparation	10 m
Cooking	10 m
Total Time	20 m

Nutritional Information:

Calories	41 kcal
Fat	0.1 g
Carbohydrates	10.3g
Protein	0.8 g
Cholesterol	0 mg
Sodium	17 mg

* Percent Daily Values are based on a 2,000 calorie diet.

CHIPOTLE CORN SALSA

Ingredients

- cooking spray
- 2 C. frozen corn
- 2 vine-ripened tomatoes, cut into 1/2 inch pieces
- 1 small red onion, diced
- 3/4 C. diced red bell pepper
- 2 jalapeno peppers - seeds removed and reserved, flesh minced
- 2 tsps finely chopped canned chipotle pepper
- 4 tbsps fresh lime juice
- 1 tbsp olive oil
- 1/4 C. chopped fresh cilantro
- salt to taste

Directions

- Heat a lightly greased large skillet on medium-high heat.
- Cook the corn till browned, stirring occasionally and transfer into a large bowl.
- Add the remaining the ingredients and stir to combine and serve.

Amount per serving (20 total)

Timing Information:

Preparation	15 m
Cooking	10 m
Total Time	25 m

Nutritional Information:

Calories	28 kcal
Fat	0.9 g
Carbohydrates	5.1g
Protein	0.8 g
Cholesterol	0 mg
Sodium	4 mg

* Percent Daily Values are based on a 2,000 calorie diet.

JALAPENO SPREAD

Ingredients

- 2 (8 oz.) packages cream cheese, softened
- 1 C. mayonnaise
- 1 (4 oz.) can chopped green chilies, drained
- 2 oz. canned diced jalapeno peppers, drained
- 1 C. grated Parmesan cheese

Directions

- In a large microwave safe bowl, add the mayonnaise and cream cheese and mix well.
- Stir in the jalapeño peppers and green chiles and top with the Parmesan.
- Microwave on high for about 3 minutes.

Amount per serving (32 total)

Timing Information:

Preparation	10 m
Cooking	3 m
Total Time	13 m

Nutritional Information:

Calories	110 kcal
Fat	11.1 g
Carbohydrates	1g
Protein	2.1 g
Cholesterol	20 mg
Sodium	189 mg

* Percent Daily Values are based on a 2,000 calorie diet.

JALAPEÑO AND BERRY JAM

Ingredients

- 4 C. crushed strawberries
- 1 C. minced jalapeno peppers
- 1/4 C. lemon juice
- 1 (2 oz.) package powdered fruit pectin
- 7 C. white sugar
- 8 half pint canning jars with lids and rings, sterilized

Directions

- In a large pan, mix together the jalapeño peppers, crushed strawberries, pectin and lemon juice on high heat and bring to a boil.
- Add the sugar and stir till it dissolves completely.
- Again bring everything to a boil and cook for about 1 minute.
- Transfer the jam into hot sterilized jars, leaving about 1/4-inch space from the top.
- Remove the bubbles from the jam by running a knife in the jars.
- Seal the jars and process in hot water bath.

Amount per serving (64 total)

Timing Information:

Preparation	40 m
Cooking	20 m
Total Time	9 h

Nutritional Information:

Calories	90 kcal
Fat	0.1 g
Carbohydrates	23.1g
Protein	0.1 g
Cholesterol	0 mg
Sodium	1 mg

* Percent Daily Values are based on a 2,000 calorie diet.

CREAMY JALAPEÑO SOUP

Ingredients

- 6 C. chicken broth
- 2 C. chopped celery
- 2 C. chopped onion
- 1 tsp garlic salt
- 2 lb. cubed Cheddar cheese
- 1 C. diced jalapeno chile pepper

Directions

- In a large pan, mix together the onion, celery, garlic salt and broth on high heat and cook for about 10 minutes.
- Remove everything from the heat and transfer everything to a blender with the cheese and pulse till smooth.
- Place the soup mixture in the pan on medium heat.
- Stir in the jalapeño peppers and cook till heated completely.

Amount per serving (6 total)

Timing Information:

Preparation	15 m
Cooking	20 m
Total Time	35 m

Nutritional Information:

Calories	644 kcal
Fat	50.4 g
Carbohydrates	9.6g
Protein	38.9 g
Cholesterol	159 mg
Sodium	1273 mg

* Percent Daily Values are based on a 2,000 calorie diet.

TEXAS JALAPEÑO CHUTNEY

Ingredients

- 5 peaches, ripe
- 2 jalapenos, stems removed, diced
- 1 tbsp ginger, finely diced
- 1 tbsp sugar
- 1 tsp ground cinnamon
- 2 tsp lemon juice

Directions

- Peel the peaches then remove the pit and chop 3 of them in a bowl.
- In a blender, add the remaining peaches and pulse till a puree forms.
- In a pan, mix together the peach puree, ginger, jalapeños, sugar, lemon juice and cinnamon on medium heat.
- Simmer, stirring occasionally for about 5-6 minutes.
- Stir in the chopped peaches and simmer everything, while stirring occasionally for about 3 minutes or till desired thickness of chutney.
- Remove everything from the heat and let it cool before serving.

Amount per serving: 6

Timing Information:

Preparation	10 mins
Total Time	20 mins

Nutritional Information:

Calories	45.9
Fat	0.3g
Cholesterol	0.0mg
Sodium	0.4mg
Carbohydrates	11.2g
Protein	0.9g

* Percent Daily Values are based on a 2,000 calorie diet.

MEDITERRANEAN CHICKPEA SOUP

Ingredients

- 2 tbsp olive oil
- 5 cloves garlic, minced
- 2 jalapeno peppers, minced
- 1 tsp ground caraway
- 1 tsp dried oregano
- 2 (14 oz.) cans chickpeas, drained and rinsed
- 2 (14 oz.) cans vegetable broth
- 2 C. water
- 5 tbsp fresh lemon juice
- 1/3 C. fresh cilantro, chopped
- salt and pepper

Directions

- In a large soup pan, heat the oil on medium heat and sauté the jalapeños and garlic till golden brown.
- Stir in the oregano and caraway seeds and sauté for a couple minutes.
- Stir in the chickpeas, water and broth and simmer everything for about 20 minutes.

- Stir in the seasoning, cilantro and lemon juice and simmer everything for about 5 minutes.

Amount per serving: 8

Timing Information:

Preparation	10 mins
Total Time	40 mins

Nutritional Information:

Calories	155.4
Fat	4.5g
Cholesterol	0.0mg
Sodium	298.7mg
Carbohydrates	24.3g
Protein	5.1g

* Percent Daily Values are based on a 2,000 calorie diet.

EASY DAHL

Ingredients

- 1 C. red lentils
- 2 tbsps ginger root, minced
- 1 tsp mustard seed
- 2 tbsps chopped fresh cilantro
- 4 tomatoes, chopped
- 3 onions, chopped
- 3 jalapeno peppers, seeded and minced
- 1 tbsp ground cumin
- 1 tbsp ground coriander seed
- 6 cloves garlic, minced
- 2 tbsps olive oil
- 1 C. water
- salt to taste

Directions

- Pressure cook the lentils until tender or boil them in water for 22 mins.
- Stir fry your mustard seeds until they being to pop then add in your oil, garlic, onions, jalapenos, and ginger.
- Continue stirring and frying until the onions are browned.

- Now pour in your tomatoes, cumin, and coriander.
- Cook the tomatoes for 2 mins and then add in your water and boil everything for 7 mins.
- Combine in your cooked lentils and mix everything.
- Finally add your preferred amount of salt.
- Serve with cilantro.
- Enjoy with cooked basmati.

Amount per serving (6 total)

Timing Information:

Preparation	Cooking	Total Time
10 m	40 m	50 m

Nutritional Information:

Calories	209 kcal
Fat	5.7 g
Carbohydrates	30.6g
Protein	10.4 g
Cholesterol	0 mg
Sodium	12 mg

* Percent Daily Values are based on a 2,000 calorie diet.

CAMBODIAN CURRY SAUCE

Ingredients

- 1/3 C. lemongrass
- 4 garlic cloves
- 1 tsp galangal, dried
- 1 tsp ground turmeric
- 1 jalapeno chili, stemmed & seeded
- 3 shallots
- 3 1/2 C. coconut milk
- 3 kaffir lime leaves
- 1 pinch salt

Directions

- In a food processor, add the lemongrass, shallots, galangal, garlic and jalapeño and pulse till a puree forms.
- In a pan, add the coconut milk and bring to a boil, then stir in the pureed mixture.
- Add the salt and lime leaves and boil, stirring continuously for about 5 minutes.
- Reduce the heat to low and simmer for about 30 minutes, stirring occasionally.
- Discard the lime leaves.

- For 1 serving, add 1/2 C. of this curry sauce into a shallow pan.
- Add 1/2 C. of the meat or vegetables and bring to a medium boil and cook to desired doneness.

Amount per serving: 1

Timing Information:

Preparation	5 mins
Total Time	45 mins

Nutritional Information:

Calories	3796.8
Fat	169.4g
Cholesterol	0.0mg
Sodium	540.0mg
Carbohydrates	574.1g
Protein	15.1g

* Percent Daily Values are based on a 2,000 calorie diet.

JALAPENO GAZPACHO

Ingredients

- 2 C. shredded zucchini
- 1 onion, coarsely diced
- 1 avocado - peeled, pitted, and coarsely diced
- 1/2 C. canned garbanzo beans, drained
- 1/4 C. apple cider vinegar
- 1 jalapeno pepper, seeded and minced
- 2 tsps lemon juice (optional)
- 1 clove garlic, smashed
- 1/4 tsp salt, or more to taste
- 1/4 tsp ground black pepper, or more to taste

Directions

- Get a bowl, combine: pepper, zucchini, garlic, salt, onions, lemon juice, avocado, jalapeno, garbanzos, and cider vinegar.
- Stir the mix to evenly distribute the contents and place a covering of plastic around the bowl.
- Put everything in the fridge for 2 hrs.
- Enjoy.

Amount per serving (4 total)

Timing Information:

Preparation	
Cooking	20 m
Total Time	2 h 20 m

Nutritional Information:

Calories	155 kcal
Fat	7.9 g
Carbohydrates	19.4g
Protein	4 g
Cholesterol	0 mg
Sodium	248 mg

* Percent Daily Values are based on a 2,000 calorie diet

Avocado Salsa

Ingredients

- 1 mango, peeled, seeded and diced
- 1 avocado, peeled, pitted, and diced
- 4 medium tomatoes, diced
- 1 jalapeno pepper, seeded and diced
- 1/2 C. chopped fresh cilantro
- 3 cloves garlic, diced
- 1 tsp salt
- 2 tbsps fresh lime juice
- 1/4 C. chopped red onion
- 3 tbsps olive oil

Directions

- Get a bowl, mix: garlic, mango, cilantro, avocado, and tomatoes.
- Stir the mix then add in your olive oil, salt, red onions, and lime juice.
- Stir your salsa to evenly distribute the liquids. Then place a covering of plastic on the bowl and put everything in the fridge for 40 mins.
- Enjoy.

Amount per serving (6 total)

Timing Information:

Preparation	
Cooking	15 m
Total Time	45 m

Nutritional Information:

Calories	158 kcal
Fat	12 g
Carbohydrates	13.8g
Protein	1.9 g
Cholesterol	0 mg
Sodium	397 mg

* Percent Daily Values are based on a 2,000 calorie diet.

New World Ceviche

Ingredients

- 1 (16 oz.) package cooked medium shrimp, peeled and deveined
- 2 (8 oz.) packages imitation crabmeat, cut into 1-inch pieces
- 5 tomatoes, diced
- 3 avocados, peeled and diced
- 1 English cucumber, peeled and cut into bite-size pieces
- 1 red onion, diced
- 1 bunch cilantro, chopped, or more to taste
- 4 limes, juiced
- 2 jalapeno peppers, seeded and finely diced
- 2 cloves garlic, pressed
- 1 (64 oz.) bottle tomato and clam juice cocktail
- salt and ground black pepper to taste

Directions

- Get a bowl, combine: garlic, crab, jalapeno, tomatoes, lime juice, avocados, shrimp, cilantro, cucumber, and red onions.
- Stir the mix then add in the clam juice cocktail.

- Stir the mix again then place a covering of plastic on the bowl and put everything in the fridge for 8 hrs.
- Enjoy.

Amount per serving (20 total)

Timing Information:

Preparation	
Cooking	1 h
Total Time	9 h

Nutritional Information:

Calories	152 kcal
Fat	4.9 g
Carbohydrates	19.7g
Protein	8.3 g
Cholesterol	49 mg
Sodium	597 mg

* Percent Daily Values are based on a 2,000 calorie diet.

Salsa Verde

(Green Salsa from Morelos)

Ingredients:

- 2 pounds tomatillos, husked
- 2 fresh jalapeno peppers
- 3 cloves garlic, peeled
- 1 dash cloves
- 1/2 tsp ground cumin
- 1 dash black pepper
- 1 tsp chicken bouillon granules, or salt

Directions:

- Cook tomatillos, jalapenos and garlic in a large sized pan after putting in water.
- Now bring this to a boil and cook for about 10 minutes or until the color of the tomatillos turn yellow after turning down the heat to medium.
- Allow it to cool down for 10 minutes and after removing all the water from; put these tomatillos, along with cloves, pepper, cumin and chicken bouillon into the blender.
- Blend until the required smoothness is achieved.
- Serve.

Serving: 1 quart

Timing Information:

Preparation	Cooking	Total Time
10 min	10 min	30 min

Nutritional Information:

Calories	20 kcal
Carbohydrates	3.7 g
Cholesterol	< 1 mg
Fat	0.6 g
Fiber	1.2 g
Protein	0.6 g
Sodium	24 mg

* Percent Daily Values are based on a 2,000 calorie diet.

ITALIAN COUNTRYSIDE SPREAD

Ingredients

- 2 (8 oz.) packages cream cheese, softened
- 2 tsp chopped garlic
- 1 tsp salt
- 1 (14 oz.) can artichoke hearts, drained and chopped
- 1/3 C. chopped black olives
- 8 green onions, chopped
- 3 oz. sun-dried tomatoes, softened and chopped
- 1/4 C. chopped parsley
- 1 tbsp chopped fresh chives

Directions

- In a bowl, mix together the cream cheese, salt and garlic.
- Fold in the remaining ingredients.
- Refrigerate for overnight before serving.

Amount per serving (6 total)

Timing Information:

Preparation	20 m
Cooking	10 m
Total Time	30 m

Nutritional Information:

Calories	365 kcal
Fat	27.4 g
Carbohydrates	20.8g
Protein	11.4 g
Cholesterol	82 mg
Sodium	1092 mg

* Percent Daily Values are based on a 2,000 calorie diet.

ENJOYABLE FRUIT DIP

Ingredients

- 1 (8 oz.) package cream cheese, softened
- 1 C. brown sugar
- 1 tbsp vanilla extract

Directions

- In a bowl, add the cream cheese and beat till whipped.
- Add the vanilla and brown sugar and beat till well combined.

Amount per serving (8 total)

Timing Information:

Preparation	10 m
Total Time	10 m

Nutritional Information:

Calories	171 kcal
Fat	9.8 g
Cholesterol	18.7g
Sodium	2.1 g
Carbohydrates	31 mg
Protein	88 mg

* Percent Daily Values are based on a 2,000 calorie diet.

TRADITIONAL LEBANESE STYLE CREAM CHEESE

Ingredients

- 16 C. plain yogurt
- 1 tsp salt, or to taste
- 1/4 C. olive oil

Directions

- Place a cheesecloth in a colander and arrange the colander in a sink.
- Add the salt into yogurt and mix well.
- Place the yogurt into the colander and keep aside for about 24 hours.
- Transfer the cheese into a bowl and stir in the olive oil.
- Transfer the cheese into a airtight container and store

Amount per serving (32 total)

Timing Information:

Preparation	5 m
Cooking	1 d
Total Time	1 d 5 m

Nutritional Information:

Calories	92 kcal
Fat	3.6 g
Carbohydrates	8.6g
Protein	6.4 g
Cholesterol	7 mg
Sodium	158 mg

* Percent Daily Values are based on a 2,000 calorie diet.

Hearty Veggie Soup

Ingredients

- 2 (29 oz.) cans diced tomatoes with liquid
- 2 stalks celery, chopped
- 2 cloves garlic, minced
- 1 red bell pepper, chopped
- 2 tbsp margarine
- 1/2 lb. mushrooms, chopped
- 1 onion, finely diced
- 2 tbsp all-purpose flour
- 1 tsp white sugar
- 8 C. beef stock
- 1/2 tsp dried basil
- 1/2 tsp dried rosemary
- 1/2 tsp dried thyme
- 1 (3 oz.) package cream cheese
- salt and pepper to taste
- 3 tbsp chopped fresh parsley

Directions

- Set your oven to 325 degrees F before doing anything else and grease a baking dish.
- In the prepared baking dish, mix together the tomatoes with the liquid, red pepper, celery and garlic.
- Cover the baking dish and cook everything in the oven for about 25 minutes.

- In a large soup pan, melt the margarine on medium heat and sauté the mushrooms and onions for about 8 minutes.
- Slowly, add the flour and sugar, stirring continuously.
- Add the beef broth and herbs and bring to a boil, stirring continuously.
- Add the baked vegetables and bring to a boil.
- Simmer, covered for about 30 minutes.
- Meanwhile, in a food processor, add the cream cheese, salt and black pepper and pulse till smooth.
- Slowly stir the cream cheese mixture into the soup.
- Serve with a garnishing of the parsley.

Amount per serving (11 total)

Timing Information:

Preparation	30 m
Total Time	30 m

Nutritional Information:

Calories	127 kcal
Fat	5.6 g
Cholesterol	11.8g
Sodium	5.9 g
Carbohydrates	8 mg
Protein	463 mg

* Percent Daily Values are based on a 2,000 calorie diet.

APPLE BUTTER SPREAD

Ingredients

- 1 (8 oz.) package light cream cheese, softened
- 1/2 C. apple butter
- 1/2 tsp vanilla extract
- 1 pinch ground cinnamon

Directions

- In a food processor, add all the ingredients and pulse till smooth.
- Transfer the spread into a bowl and refrigerate, covered for about 30 minutes.

Amount per serving (12 total)

Timing Information:

Preparation	5 m
Cooking	35 m
Total Time	40 m

Nutritional Information:

Calories	65 kcal
Fat	3.4 g
Carbohydrates	6.4g
Protein	2.1 g
Cholesterol	11 mg
Sodium	58 mg

* Percent Daily Values are based on a 2,000 calorie diet.

MEXICAN THEMED SALSA

Ingredients

- 1 mango - peeled, seeded, and chopped
- 1/4 C. finely chopped red bell pepper
- 1 green onion, chopped
- 2 tbsp chopped cilantro
- 1 fresh jalapeno chili pepper, finely chopped
- 2 tbsp lime juice
- 1 tbsp lemon juice

Directions

- In a bowl, mix together all the ingredients.
- Cover and keep aside for about 30 minutes.

Amount per serving (8 total)

Timing Information:

Preparation	15 m
Total Time	45 m

Nutritional Information:

Calories	21 kcal
Fat	0.1 g
Cholesterol	5.4g
Sodium	0.3 g
Carbohydrates	0 mg
Protein	1 mg

* Percent Daily Values are based on a 2,000 calorie diet.

HOMEMADE DELICIOUS MANGO JAM

Ingredients

- 2 lb. ripe mangoes
- 1 1/2 C. white sugar
- 3/4 C. water
- 3 saffron threads

Directions

- Microwave the whole mangoes till soft and keep aside to cool completely.
- Remove the peel and pit from the mangoes.
- In a bowl, add the pulp and mash it.
- In a large pan, mix together the water and sugar on low heat.
- Bring to a boil, stirring occasionally.
- Increase the heat to medium-high and boil till the soft threads form.
- Stir in the mango pulp and saffron threads and boil for about 5 minutes, stirring occasionally.
- Transfer the jam into sterilized jars and seal according to canning directions.

Amount per serving (24 total)

Timing Information:

Preparation	15 m
Cooking	45 m
Total Time	1 h

Nutritional Information:

Calories	73 kcal
Fat	0.1 g
Carbohydrates	18.9g
Protein	0.2 g
Cholesterol	0 mg
Sodium	1 mg

* Percent Daily Values are based on a 2,000 calorie diet.

REFRESHING MANGO RELISH

Ingredients

- 1 mango - peeled, seeded and diced
- 1 tsp extra virgin olive oil
- 1/2 red bell pepper, chopped
- 2 green onion, thinly sliced
- 1 tbsp chopped cilantro
- 1 lime, juiced
- 1/4 tsp salt
- 1 pinch cracked black pepper
- 1 tsp honey

Directions

- In a bowl, mix together all the ingredients.
- Serve immediately or this relish can be served chilled.

Amount per serving (4 total)

Timing Information:

Preparation	15 m
Cooking	15 m
Total Time	30 m

Nutritional Information:

Calories	63 kcal
Fat	1.4 g
Carbohydrates	13.7g
Protein	0.7 g
Cholesterol	0 mg
Sodium	149 mg

* Percent Daily Values are based on a 2,000 calorie diet.

Chunky Guacamole

Ingredients

- 2 tbsp minced white onion
- 2 limes, juiced
- 2 serrano chili peppers
- 2 limes, juiced
- sea salt to taste
- 4 ripe avocados, peeled and pitted
- 1/4 C. chopped fresh cilantro
- 1 large mango - peeled, seeded, and chopped

Directions

- In a bowl, mix together the juice of the 2 limes and onion and keep aside for about 1 hour.
- Strain well and squeezes to remove the extra juice, then keep aside.
- In a food processor, add the juice of the 2 limes, Serrano Chili and salt and pulse till chopped finely.
- Add the avocado and pulse till smooth.
- Transfer the mixture into a serving bowl.
- Add the onion, mango and cilantro and stir to combine.
- Serve immediately.

Amount per serving (8 total)

Timing Information:

Preparation	20 m
Total Time	20 m

Nutritional Information:

Calories	198 kcal
Fat	14.9 g
Cholesterol	19g
Sodium	2.5 g
Carbohydrates	0 mg
Protein	49 mg

* Percent Daily Values are based on a 2,000 calorie diet.

COLORFUL CEVICHE

Ingredients

- 3 mangos - peeled, seeded, and diced
- 1 yellow onion, diced
- 1 green bell pepper, diced
- 1 red bell pepper, diced
- 3 jalapeno peppers, minced
- 1/2 bunch fresh cilantro, minced
- 2 limes, juiced (with pulp)

Directions

- I a bowl, mix together all the ingredients.
- Refrigerate, covered for about 1 hour.

Amount per serving (6 total)

Timing Information:

Preparation	20 m
Total Time	1 h 20 m

Nutritional Information:

Calories	80 kcal
Fat	0.4 g
Cholesterol	20.1g
Sodium	1.4 g
Carbohydrates	0 mg
Protein	7 mg

* Percent Daily Values are based on a 2,000 calorie diet.

Velvety Mango Mousse

Ingredients

- 1 C. heavy whipping cream
- 1 C. mango, pureed

Directions

- In a glass bowl, add the cream and beat till stiff peaks form.
- The whipped cream will form sharp peaks by lifting the beater straight up.
- Fold in the mango puree and transfer into serving glasses.
- Refrigerate to chill for about 3 hours.

Amount per serving (4 total)

Timing Information:

Preparation	15 m
Total Time	3 h 15 m

Nutritional Information:

Calories	232 kcal
Fat	22.1 g
Cholesterol	8.7g
Sodium	1.4 g
Carbohydrates	82 mg
Protein	23 mg

* Percent Daily Values are based on a 2,000 calorie diet.

Warm Mango Sauce

Ingredients

- 3 C. mangos, peeled, seeded and chopped
- 1 tbsp butter
- 1 tbsp brown sugar
- 1 tsp lemon juice
- 1 tsp orange juice
- 3 tbsp water

Directions

- In a pan, add all the ingredients on medium heat and cook stirring till the mixture becomes thick.
- Remove everything from the heat and serve.

Amount per serving (4 total)

Timing Information:

Preparation	10 m
Cooking	15 m
Total Time	25 m

Nutritional Information:

Calories	120 kcal
Fat	3.2 g
Carbohydrates	24.6g
Protein	0.7 g
Cholesterol	8 mg
Sodium	24 mg

* Percent Daily Values are based on a 2,000 calorie diet.

Bright Summertime Gazpacho

Ingredients

- 2 C. 1/4-inch-diced fresh mangoes
- 2 C. orange juice
- 2 tbsp extra-virgin olive oil
- 1 seedless cucumber, cut into 1/4-inch dice
- 1 small red bell pepper, seeded and cut into 1/4-inch dice
- 1 small onion, cut into 1/4-inch dice
- 2 medium garlic cloves, minced
- 1 small jalapeno pepper, seeded and minced
- 3 tbsp fresh lime juice
- 2 tbsp chopped fresh parsley
- Salt and freshly ground black pepper

Directions

- In a blender, add the mangoes, oil and orange juice and pulse till pureed.
- Transfer the mango puree in a bowl with the remaining all ingredients and mix well.
- Refrigerate till serving.

Amount per serving (6 total)

Timing Information:

Preparation	20 m
Total Time	20 m

Nutritional Information:

Calories	147 kcal
Fat	5 g
Cholesterol	26.2g
Sodium	1.6 g
Carbohydrates	0 mg
Protein	5 mg

* Percent Daily Values are based on a 2,000 calorie diet.

INDIAN MANGO CHUTNEY

Ingredients

- 3 C. distilled white vinegar
- 6 C. white sugar
- 6 C. brown sugar
- 1 tsp ground cinnamon
- 2 tsp ground ginger
- 4 tsp ground allspice
- 1 tsp ground cloves
- 2 tsp ground nutmeg
- 5 small red hot chili peppers, seeded and chopped
- 1 tsp kosher salt
- 2 large onions, chopped
- 3 cloves garlic, chopped
- 1 C. golden raisins
- 1 C. raisins
- 1/2 C. fresh ginger root, chopped
- 16 C. sliced, semi-ripe mangos
- 1/2 C. sliced almonds

Directions

- In a large pan, mix together the chili peppers, vinegar, both the sugars, spices and salt and bring to a boil.
- Cook for about 30 minutes.
- Stir in the remaining ingredients except the mangoes and almonds and cook for about 30 minutes.

- Reduce the heat to low and stir in the mangoes and almonds then simmer for about 30 minutes.
- Transfer the mixture into the sterilized jars, about 1/2-inch below from the top, then seal tightly.

Amount per serving (240 total)

Timing Information:

Preparation	10 m
Cooking	1 h 30 m
Total Time	1 h 40 m

Nutritional Information:

Calories	46 kcal
Fat	0.2 g
Carbohydrates	11.6g
Protein	0.2 g
Cholesterol	0 mg
Sodium	13 mg

* Percent Daily Values are based on a 2,000 calorie diet.

EASTERN SPANISH AIOLI

INGREDIENTS

- 3/4 C. mayonnaise
- 3 garlic cloves, minced
- 1 tbsp fresh lemon juice
- 1 tbsp balsamic vinegar
- 2 tsp chopped fresh rosemary

Directions

- In a bowl, add all the ingredients and beat well.
- Refrigerate, covered before serving.

Amount per serving: 1

Timing Information:

Preparation	5 mins
Total Time	5 mins

Nutritional Information:

Calories	44.1
Fat	3.6g
Cholesterol	2.8mg
Sodium	78.4mg
Carbohydrates	2.9g
Protein	0.1g

* Percent Daily Values are based on a 2,000 calorie diet.

El Pollo Soup

Ingredients

- 3 cooked, boneless chicken breast halves, shredded
- 1 (15 oz.) can kidney beans
- 1 C. whole kernel corn
- 1 (14.5 oz.) can stewed tomatoes
- 1/2 C. chopped onion
- 1/2 green bell pepper, chopped
- 1/2 red bell pepper, chopped
- 1 (4 oz.) can chopped green chili peppers
- 2 (14.5 oz.) cans chicken broth
- 1 tbsp ground cumin

Directions

- In a large pan mix together all the ingredients on medium heat.
- Simmer for about 45 minutes.

Amount per serving (4 total)

Timing Information:

Preparation	20 m
Cooking	45 m
Total Time	1 h 5 m

Nutritional Information:

Calories	335 kcal
Fat	7.7 g
Carbohydrates	37.7g
Protein	31.5 g
Cholesterol	62 mg
Sodium	841 mg

* Percent Daily Values are based on a 2,000 calorie diet.

GROUND BEEF MEXICAN DIP

Ingredients

- 1 lb. ground beef
- 1 (16 oz.) jar salsa
- 1 (10.75 oz.) can condensed cream of mushroom soup
- 2 lb. processed cheese food, cubed

Directions

- Heat a medium pan on medium-high heat and cook the beef till browned completely.
- Drain off the grease from the pan.
- In a slow cooker, transfer the cooked beef with the salsa, condensed cream of mushroom soup and processed cheese food.
- Set the slow cooker on High till cheese melts completely.
- Now, set the slow cooker on Low and simmer till serving.

Amount per serving (32 total)

Timing Information:

Preparation	25 m
Cooking	25 m
Total Time	50 m

Nutritional Information:

Calories	150 kcal
Fat	11.3 g
Carbohydrates	3.9g
Protein	8.3 g
Cholesterol	30 mg
Sodium	429 mg

* Percent Daily Values are based on a 2,000 calorie diet.

Mexican Veggie Puree

Ingredients

- 6 spears fresh asparagus, trimmed and cut into 1/2 inch pieces
- 1 C. bite-size cauliflower florets
- 2 stalks celery ribs, chopped
- 1/3 C. canned kidney beans, drained
- 1/3 C. chopped hazelnuts
- 2/3 tsp chopped fresh dill
- 1/4 tsp dried basil
- 1/2 tsp minced garlic
- 2 tbsp sunflower seed oil
- 1/3 tsp chili powder
- 1/4 tsp celery seed
- 1/2 tsp salt

Directions

- Steam the asparagus and cauliflower for about 10 minutes.
- Transfer the vegetables into a bowl and stir in the celery.

- In a blender, add the kidney beans, hazelnuts, dill, basil, garlic, oil, chili powder, celery seed and salt and pulse till smooth.
- Pour the sauce over the vegetables mixture and serve.

Amount per serving (4 total)

Timing Information:

Preparation	25 m
Cooking	10 m
Total Time	35 m

Nutritional Information:

Calories	167 kcal
Fat	14.1 g
Carbohydrates	8.3g
Protein	4.1 g
Cholesterol	0 mg
Sodium	363 mg

* Percent Daily Values are based on a 2,000 calorie diet.

CLASSICAL MEXICAN CEVICHE

Ingredients

- 5 large lemons, juiced
- 1 lb. jumbo shrimp, peeled and deveined
- 1/4 C. chopped fresh cilantro
- tomato and clam juice cocktail
- 2 white onions, finely chopped
- 1 cucumber, peeled and finely chopped
- 1 large tomatoes, seeded and chopped
- 3 fresh jalapeno peppers, seeded and minced
- 1 bunch radishes, finely diced
- 2 cloves fresh garlic, minced
- tortilla chips

Directions

- In a bowl, add the shrimp and enough lemon juice to cover the shrimp completely.
- Refrigerate, covered for about 30 minutes.
- Remove the bowl of shrimp from the refrigerator.
- Add the tomatoes, onions, cucumber, radishes and garlic and toss to coat.
- Slowly, stir in the cilantro and jalapeño peppers.

- Stir in the tomato and clam juice and refrigerate, covered for about 1 hour.
- Serve chilled with the tortilla chips.

Amount per serving (8 total)

Timing Information:

Preparation	30 m
Cooking	30 m
Total Time	2 h

Nutritional Information:

Calories	387 kcal
Fat	12.4 g
Carbohydrates	57.6g
Protein	17.7 g
Cholesterol	86 mg
Sodium	733 mg

* Percent Daily Values are based on a 2,000 calorie diet.

GUACAMOLE 101

Ingredients

- 3 avocados, peeled and mashed
- 1 red onion, minced
- 1 red bell pepper, chopped
- 1/2 yellow bell pepper, chopped
- 1 green bell pepper, chopped
- 1 fresh jalapeno pepper, chopped
- 1/3 C. chopped fresh cilantro
- 1 lime, juiced

Directions

- In a large bowl, add all the ingredients and mix well.
- Refrigerate, covered before serving.

Amount per serving (3 total)

Timing Information:

Preparation	10 m
Total Time	10 m

Nutritional Information:

Calories	371 kcal
Fat	29.8 g
Cholesterol	28.9g
Sodium	5.7 g
Carbohydrates	0 mg
Protein	22 mg

* Percent Daily Values are based on a 2,000 calorie diet.

GUADALAJARA GRAVY

Ingredients

- 1/2 C. flour
- 2 tbsp chili powder
- 2 tsp onion powder
- 1 tsp dried Mexican oregano
- 1 tsp salt
- 6 tbsp vegetable oil
- 4 C. water

Directions

- In a bowl, mix together the flour, chili powder, onion powder, oregano and salt.
- In a large pan, heat the oil on low heat.
- Slowly, add the flour mixture, beating continuously till smooth.
- Slowly, add the water, beating continuously till smooth and bring to a gentle simmer.
- Simmer for about 5 minutes.
- Remove from the heat and cool for about 10 minutes.

Amount per serving (6 total)

Timing Information:

Preparation	10 m
Cooking	10 m
Total Time	30 m

Nutritional Information:

Calories	170 kcal
Fat	14.2 g
Carbohydrates	10.1g
Protein	1.5 g
Cholesterol	0 mg
Sodium	420 mg

* Percent Daily Values are based on a 2,000 calorie diet.

Pumpkin Soup I

Ingredients:

- 2 small sugar pumpkins, halved and seeded
- 3 C. chicken broth
- ¾ C. heavy whipping cream
- ½ tsp ground sage, crushed
- ¼ tsp ground nutmeg
- 1½ tsp salt
- ¼ C. sour cream

Directions:

- Set your oven to 400 degrees F. Grease baking sheet.
- Place pumpkin, cut side down onto prepared baking sheet.
- Roast for about 45 minutes. Remove the pumpkin from oven and let it cool completely.
- After cooling, scrape out the flesh of pumpkin.
- In a food processor, add pumpkin flesh and broth and pulse till smooth.
- Transfer the pureed soup in a large pan on medium heat.
- Bring to a gentle simmer. Then, stir in whipping cream, sage, nutmeg and salt till well combined.
- Transfer the soup in serving bowls.

- Top with the dollop of sour cream and serve hot.

Amount per serving (4 total)

Timing Information:

Preparation	Cooking	Total Time
15 minutes	50-55 minutes	1 hour 10 minutes

Nutritional Information:

Calories	245
Fat	19.8g
Cholesterol	67mg
Sodium	899mg
Carbohydrates	16.8g
Fiber	1.2g
Protein	3.7g

* Percent Daily Values are based on a 2,000 calorie diet.

APPLE SOUP FOR COLD FALL NIGHTS

Ingredients

- 1 tbsp reduced-fat margarine
- 3 tart apples - peeled, cored, and chopped
- 3 pears - peeled, cored, and chopped
- 5 C. vegetable broth
- 1/2 tsp rubbed sage
- 1/4 tsp ground black pepper
- 1 bay leaf
- 1 1/2 tsp pureed fresh ginger
- 1 tbsp chopped fresh parsley

Directions

- In a large pan, melt the margarine on medium heat and cook the apples and peas for about 5 minutes.
- Add the broth, sage, bay leaf and pepper and bring everything to a boil.
- Reduce the heat to low and simmer, covered for about 20 minutes.
- Remove everything from the heat and keep aside for about 5 minutes to cool.

- In a blender, add the soup mixture in batches and pulse till smooth.
- Return the soup in the pan on medium heat and cook till heated completely.
- Serve with a topping of parsley.

Amount per serving (7 total)

Timing Information:

Preparation	20 m
Cooking	35 m
Total Time	1 h

Nutritional Information:

Calories	102 kcal
Fat	1.3 g
Carbohydrates	22.9g
Protein	1.2 g
Cholesterol	0 mg
Sodium	349 mg

* Percent Daily Values are based on a 2,000 calorie diet.

CREAMY AVOCADO STEW

Ingredients

- 2 avocado, peeled, pitted and diced
- 1 tbsp chopped shallots
- 1 tbsp olive oil
- 2 C. chicken stock
- 1 C. heavy cream
- salt and pepper to taste
- 1/4 tsp ground nutmeg
- 1 tomato, peeled, seeded and diced

Directions

- Add your avocado to the bowl of a food processor and begin to puree it.
- Begin to stir fry your shallots in olive oil until they are soft then shut the heat.
- Get a bowl, combine: chicken stock, shallots, cream, and avocado.
- Stir the mix until it is smooth then add in the nutmeg, some pepper and salt.
- Place a covering of plastic on the bowl and put the mix in the fridge for 30 mins.

- When serving the dish top the soup with your tomatoes.
- Enjoy.

Amount per serving (4 total)

Timing Information:

Preparation	15 m
Cooking	10 m
Total Time	55 m

Nutritional Information:

Calories	410 kcal
Fat	40.6 g
Carbohydrates	12.5g
Protein	3.9 g
Cholesterol	82 mg
Sodium	374 mg

* Percent Daily Values are based on a 2,000 calorie diet.

BIG APPLE SOUP

Ingredients

- 3 tbsps olive oil
- 1 shallot, minced
- 2 small apples, peeled, cored, and diced
- 4 C. vegetable broth
- 2 C. water
- 1/2 tsp freshly grated nutmeg
- 1/2 tsp ground allspice
- 1/2 tsp ground cinnamon
- 1/4 tsp coarsely ground black pepper
- 1 (12 oz.) box frozen butternut squash
- 1/2 C. half-and-half
- 2 tbsps butter
- 1/2 tsp dried tarragon

Directions

- Stir fry your shallots in olive oil until they are soft then add in the apples and fry them for 2 mins.
- Place everything into a large pot and add in the water and broth to the pot and stir the mix.
- Now add in: the pepper, nutmeg, cinnamon, and allspice.

- Get everything boiling, set the heat to low, and let the mix cook for 20 mins.
- Add the squash to the soup and get everything boiling again.
- Add the half and half and the tarragon as well and let the mix cook for 7 mins.
- Enjoy.

Amount per serving (8 total)

Timing Information:

Preparation	10 m
Cooking	25 m
Total Time	35 m

Nutritional Information:

Calories	143 kcal
Fat	10.1 g
Carbohydrates	12.7g
Protein	2 g
Cholesterol	16 mg
Sodium	662 mg

* Percent Daily Values are based on a 2,000 calorie diet.

BALSAMIC GAZPACHO

Ingredients

- 6 medium ripe tomatoes, diced
- 2 cucumbers, peeled and finely chopped
- 1 onion, diced
- 1 green bell pepper, diced
- jalapeno pepper, seeded and diced
- 1 large lemon, juiced
- 1 tbsp balsamic vinegar
- 2 tsps olive oil
- 1 tsp kosher salt
- 1/2 tsp ground black pepper
- 1/4 C. chopped fresh dill

Directions

- Get a bowl, combine: jalapeno, tomatoes, bell peppers, cucumber, and onions.
- Stir the mix then add in the pepper, lemon juice, salt, balsamic and olive oil.
- Stir the mix again then add half of the mix to the bowl of a food processor and puree it then combine in the rest of the gazpacho and puree it as well.
- Enjoy.

Amount per serving (6 total)

Timing Information:

Preparation	
Cooking	25 m
Total Time	1 h 25 m

Nutritional Information:

Calories	58 kcal
Fat	2 g
Carbohydrates	10.9g
Protein	2 g
Cholesterol	0 mg
Sodium	330 mg

* Percent Daily Values are based on a 2,000 calorie diet.

Avocado and Garlic Gazpacho

Ingredients

- 2 C. shredded zucchini
- 1 onion, coarsely chopped
- 1 avocado - peeled, pitted, and coarsely chopped
- 1/2 C. canned garbanzo beans, drained
- 1/4 C. apple cider vinegar
- 1 jalapeno pepper, seeded and diced
- 2 tsps lemon juice
- 1 clove garlic, smashed
- 1/4 tsp salt, or more to taste
- 1/4 tsp ground black pepper, or more to taste

Directions

- Get a bowl, combine: black pepper, zucchini, salt, onion, garlic, avocado, garbanzo, lemon juice, apple cider, and jalapenos.
- Stir the mix then place a covering of plastic on the bowl.
- Put everything in the fridge for 60 mins.
- Enjoy.

Amount per serving (4 total)

Timing Information:

Preparation	
Cooking	20 m
Total Time	1 h 20 m

Nutritional Information:

Calories	155 kcal
Fat	7.9 g
Carbohydrates	19.4g
Protein	4 g
Cholesterol	0 mg
Sodium	248 mg

* Percent Daily Values are based on a 2,000 calorie diet.

Southern Gazpacho

Ingredients

- 5 C. shredded green cabbage
- 1/2 C. chopped cucumber
- 1 C. chopped tomato
- 1/2 C. chopped yellow bell pepper
- 1/2 C. chopped green onions
- 1/2 C. chopped celery
- 1/4 C. tomato-vegetable juice cocktail
- 1/4 C. red wine vinegar
- 1 tsp white sugar
- 1 tbsp olive oil
- 1 tbsp salsa
- 1/2 lemon, juiced
- salt and pepper to taste

Directions

- Get a bowl, combine: celery, cabbage, green onions, cucumbers, bell peppers, and tomatoes.
- Get a 2nd bowl, combine: lemon juice, tomato juice, salsa, vinegar, olive oil, and sugar.
- Stir in some pepper and salt.

- Combine both bowls then place a covering of plastic on the bowl and put everything in the fridge for 3 hrs.
- Enjoy.

Amount per serving (6 total)

Timing Information:

Preparation	
Cooking	20 m
Total Time	2 h 20 m

Nutritional Information:

Calories	63 kcal
Fat	2.5 g
Carbohydrates	10.6g
Protein	1.9 g
Cholesterol	0 mg
Sodium	132 mg

* Percent Daily Values are based on a 2,000 calorie diet.

Sunrise Gazpacho

Ingredients

- 3 pints hulled strawberries
- 1/2 cucumber - peeled, seeded, and chopped
- 1/2 onion, chopped
- 1/4 C. chopped fresh cilantro
- 1/4 C. chopped fresh parsley
- 1 pint hulled strawberries, chopped
- 1/2 cucumber - peeled, seeded, and chopped
- 1/2 onion, chopped
- 1/4 C. chopped fresh cilantro
- 1/4 C. chopped fresh parsley
- 1 bunch green onions, diced
- 1 jalapeno pepper, seeded and diced
- 1/3 C. red wine vinegar
- 3 tbsps fresh lemon juice
- 2 tbsps olive oil
- 1 1/2 tsps salt
- 2 cloves garlic, diced
- 1 tsp dried tarragon
- 1 tsp dried basil
- 1/4 tsp hot pepper sauce
- 1/8 tsp ground black pepper
- 1 large avocado - peeled, pitted, and cubed

Directions

- Add the following to the bowl of a food processor: 1/4 C. parsley, 3 pints strawberries, 1/4 C. cilantro, half of the onion, half of the cucumber.
- Process the mix for 1 min then place everything in a bowl.
- Now add the following to the pureed mix: black pepper, 1 pint strawberries, hot sauce, 1/2 cucumber, basil, tarragon, 1/2 onion, garlic, salt, 1/4 C. cilantro, olive oil, 1/4 C. parsley, lemon juice, wine vinegar, jalapenos, and green onions.
- Top everything with the pieces of avocado then place a covering of plastic on the bowl and put the mix in the fridge for 3 hrs.
- Enjoy.

Amount per serving (6 total)

Timing Information:

Preparation	
Cooking	30 m
Total Time	2 h 30 m

Nutritional Information:

Calories	231 kcal
Fat	12.4 g
Carbohydrates	31.4g
Protein	4.2 g
Cholesterol	0 mg
Sodium	605 mg

* Percent Daily Values are based on a 2,000 calorie diet.

LIME GAZPACHO

Ingredients

- 2 C. 1/4-inch-diced fresh mangoes
- 2 C. orange juice
- 2 tbsps extra-virgin olive oil
- 1 seedless cucumber, cut into 1/4-inch dice
- 1 small red bell pepper, seeded and cut into 1/4-inch dice
- 1 small onion, cut into 1/4-inch dice
- 2 medium garlic cloves, diced
- 1 small jalapeno pepper, seeded and diced (optional)
- 3 tbsps fresh lime juice
- 2 tbsps chopped fresh parsley, basil or cilantro
- Salt and freshly ground black pepper

Directions

- Add the oil, orange juice, and mangoes to the bowl of a food processor and puree the mix.
- Place everything in a bowl then add in some pepper and salt.
- Place a covering of plastic on the bowl and put everything in the fridge for 60 mins.
- Enjoy.

PARSLEY GAZPACHO

Ingredients

- 1 (1 lb) package bacon, cut into 1-inch pieces
- 8 large ripe tomatoes, diced
- 1/2 salad cucumber, diced
- 1 onion, chopped
- 1 tbsp extra-virgin olive oil
- 1 clove garlic, diced
- 1/4 tsp dried parsley, or to taste
- salt and ground black pepper to taste

Directions

- Stir fry your bacon for 12 mins until fully done then place the bacon to the side and crumble it.
- Add the onion, cucumber, and tomatoes to a bowl of a food processor and puree the mix.
- Now begin to stir fry your garlic for 60 mins in olive oil then add the pureed mix to the oil.
- Stir everything then add in the pepper, salt, and parsley and stir everything again.
- Place a lid on the pan, set the heat to low, and let the contents cook for 1 hr.
- Top the gazpacho with the bacon.

- Enjoy.

Amount per serving (6 total)

Timing Information:

Preparation	20 m
Cooking	50 m
Total Time	1 h 10 m

Nutritional Information:

Calories	210 kcal
Fat	13.2 g
Carbohydrates	12.6g
Protein	11.7 g
Cholesterol	27 mg
Sodium	587 mg

* Percent Daily Values are based on a 2,000 calorie diet.

Cajun Bisque

Ingredients

- 3 tbsps butter
- 3 tbsps all-purpose flour
- 1 tbsp vegetable oil
- 1 large onion, chopped
- 1 tbsp diced garlic
- 1 large celery stalk, diced
- Cajun seasoning to taste
- 1 C. chicken broth
- 1 1/2 C. frozen corn kernels
- 1 bay leaf
- 2 C. milk
- 2 C. heavy cream
- 1 tsp liquid shrimp and crab boil seasoning
- 1 lb fresh lump crabmeat
- 1/4 C. chopped green onions
- 1/2 tsp Worcestershire sauce
- salt and black pepper to taste
- chopped green onions

Directions

- Heat and stir your flour and butter for 6 mins then shut the heat.
- Get a separate large pot and begin to stir fry your celery, garlic, and onion for 2 mins then combine in some Cajun spice.
- Stir the mix then add in the bay leaf, corn, and broth.
- Stir everything again.
- Now get the mix boiling, then add the crab boil, cream, and milk.
- Set the heat to low and let the mix gently cook for 9 mins.
- Begin to slowly add in the butter flour mix and combine the contents evenly.
- Keep cooking everything for 7 mins then add the Worcestershire, green onions, and crab meat.
- Add some pepper and salt.
- Enjoy.

Amount per serving (8 total)

Timing Information:

Preparation	20 m
Cooking	30 m
Total Time	50 m

Nutritional Information:

Calories	387 kcal
Fat	30.1 g
Carbohydrates	16.3g
Protein	14.8 g
Cholesterol	131 mg
Sodium	278 mg

* Percent Daily Values are based on a 2,000 calorie diet.

Baton Rouge Gravy

Ingredients

- 2 (4.5 oz.) cans chopped green chilies
- 1 1/2 tsps chicken bouillon granules
- 1 1/2 C. warm water, divided
- 1/4 C. all-purpose flour
- 1 tsp onion powder
- 1/8 tsp ground cayenne pepper, or to taste

Directions

- Begin to puree your chilies with a food processor.
- Get a large pot and get 1 C. of water and the bouillon boiling as well.
- Stir the mix until the bouillon is completely combined then add in the chilies.
- Get the mix boiling again then set the heat to a low level.
- Get a bowl, combine: flour and 1/2 C. of warm water. Once the mix is evenly combined it with the chili mix.
- Get everything boiling again, set the heat to medium, and cook everything for 6 mins.
- Now combine in the cayenne and onion powder.
- Enjoy.

Amount per serving (8 total)

Timing Information:

Preparation	5 m
Cooking	10 m
Total Time	15 m

Nutritional Information:

Calories	23 kcal
Fat	0.1 g
Carbohydrates	< 4.9g
Protein	0.8 g
Cholesterol	< 1 mg
Sodium	< 447 mg

* Percent Daily Values are based on a 2,000 calorie diet.

POTATO AND CELERY PÂTÉ

Ingredients

- 1 C. sunflower seeds
- 1/2 C. whole wheat flour
- 1/2 C. nutritional yeast
- 1/2 tsp salt
- 1/2 C. canola oil
- 2 tbsps lemon juice
- 1 potato, peeled and chopped
- 1 large carrot, peeled and sliced
- 1 onion, peeled and chopped
- 1 stalk celery, chopped
- 1 clove garlic, peeled
- 1 1/2 C. water
- 1/2 tsp dried thyme
- 1/2 tsp dried basil leaves
- 1/2 tsp dried sage
- 1/2 tsp dried savory
- 1/2 tsp ground black pepper
- 1/2 tsp ground dry mustard

Directions

- Set your oven to 350 degrees before doing anything else.
- Coat a casserole dish with the nonstick spray or oil.
- Add all the ingredients to the bowl of a food processor and puree the mix for 2 mins until it becomes a smooth paste.
- Pour the mix into the casserole and cook everything in the oven for 60 mins.

- Enjoy.

Amount per serving: 1

Timing Information:

Preparation	20 mins
Total Time	1 hr 20 mins

Nutritional Information:

Calories	1272.3
Cholesterol	0.0
Sodium	662.5mg
Carbohydrates	84.9g
Protein	42.5g

* Percent Daily Values are based on a 2,000 calorie diet.

Cucumber and Basil Pâté

Ingredients

- 1 can sardines, drained
- 1/2 lemon, juice and rind of
- 5 tbsps yoghurt, natural low-fat
- 1/4 C. low fat cottage cheese
- 1 C. cucumbers, finely chopped
- fresh basil leaf, finely chopped
- 1/4 tsp garlic salt
- fresh ground black pepper, to taste
- 4 thin slices cucumbers, made into twists, for garnish
- 4 sprigs parsley, for garnish

Directions

- Get a bowl, combine: lemon juice, lemon rind, and the sardines without the liquid.
- Mash everything with a fork until the mix is paste-like.
- Now combine in the cottage cheese and the yogurt but make sure to drain any excess liquids from each if you find extra moisture.
- Continue to mix to the cottage cheese and yogurt with the sardines then add in the basil and cucumber.

- Add in the black pepper and garlic salt.
- Divide the mix between 4 ramekins then top each with the parsley sprigs and the cucumber twist.
- Enjoy.

Amount per serving: 4

Timing Information:

Preparation	5 mins
Total Time	5 mins

Nutritional Information:

Calories	199.9
Cholesterol	41.2
Sodium	219.9
Carbohydrates	31.2g
Protein	14.4g

* Percent Daily Values are based on a 2,000 calorie diet.

LEMONY LEGUME PÂTÉ

Ingredients

- 14 oz. canned mixed beans, drained, rinsed
- 2 tbsps olive oil
- 1 lemon, juice of
- 2 cloves garlic, crushed
- 12 tbsps fresh cilantro, chopped
- 2 scallions, chopped
- salt and pepper
- shredded scallion

Directions

- Get a bowl and add in your beans.
- Grab a potato masher and mash the beans until they are smooth.
- Now combine in: the scallions, olive oil, cilantro, lemon juice, and garlic.
- Continue to work the mix until it is smooth again.
- Top everything with some pepper and salt and place the mix in a bowl.
- Place a covering of plastic on the bowl and put everything in the fridge for 35 mins.

- Remove the covering and top the pate with the scallions.
- Enjoy.

Amount per serving: 4

Timing Information:

Preparation	20 mins
Total Time	50 mins

Nutritional Information:

Calories	67.9
Cholesterol	0.0
Sodium	3.0
Carbohydrates	2.1g
Protein	0.3g

* Percent Daily Values are based on a 2,000 calorie diet.

Smoked Pâté

Ingredients

- 1 package cream cheese
- 1 whole smoked trout, skinned and deboned
- 1/4 C. low-fat sour cream
- 2 chopped green onions
- 2 tsps prepared horseradish
- 1 tbsp lemon juice
- fresh ground black pepper
- 1 tbsp dill

Directions

- Coat one fourth of the fish and place it to the side after flaking it.
- Add the rest of the ingredients to the bowl of a food processor excluding the herbs and puree the mix.
- Now add a bit more lemon juice and process the mix again.
- Add in the spices and process them for 1 more min.
- Pour everything into a bowl and place a covering of plastic on the bowl.
- Put everything in the fridge until it is chilled.

- Enjoy.

Amount per serving: 1

Timing Information:

Preparation	15 mins
Total Time	15 mins

Nutritional Information:

Calories	637.4
Cholesterol	199.3mg
Sodium	576.9mg
Carbohydrates	11.4g
Protein	11.5g

* Percent Daily Values are based on a 2,000 calorie diet.

HARD BOILED PÂTÉ

Ingredients

- 1 tbsp vegetable oil
- 1/2 C. onion, minced
- 1/2 tsp salt
- 1/4 C. walnuts, chopped
- 1 1/2 C. green beans, chopped
- 2 eggs, hard boiled
- 2 tsps lemon juice
- 1 tbsp mayonnaise
- black pepper, to taste
- 1/4 C. fresh parsley, chopped

Directions

- Begin to stir fry your salt and onions, in oil, for 12 mins.
- Combine in the beans and continue frying the mix for 9 more mins.
- Enter the entire mix into the bowl of a food processor and puree everything until it is smooth.
- Enjoy.

Amount per serving: 4

Timing Information:

Preparation	30 mins
Total Time	30 mins

Nutritional Information:

Calories	152.1
Cholesterol	106.7mg
Sodium	357.1mg
Carbohydrates	7.4g
Protein	5.3g

* Percent Daily Values are based on a 2,000 calorie diet.

PUMPERNICKEL PÂTÉ

Ingredients

- 1/2 C. diced salt pork
- 1 onion, diced
- 2 tbsps butter
- 1 chicken liver
- 2 slices pumpernickel bread
- milk
- 1/4 tsp salt
- 1/2 tsp fresh ground pepper
- 1/8 tsp nutmeg
- 1 tsp grated lemon rind
- 1/2 C. lean bacon, diced
- 2 eggs, beaten
- 8 slices lean bacon
- pumpernickel bread, slightly toasted

Directions

- Begin to stir fry your onions, and pork in butter until the onions are soft then add in half of the livers.
- Brown the livers then place a lid on the pan and cook everything for 17 mins.
- Now set your oven to 350 degrees before doing anything else.
- Place your bread in the milk and squeeze everything to get rid of excess liquids.

- Place the bread into the bowl of a food processor along with: the cooked liver and any remaining liver.
- Puree the mix until it is smooth then add in the rest of the ingredients except the bacon.
- Continue to puree everything until it is smooth and paste like.
- Pour the puree into a bread pan and top the mix with the bacon pieces.
- Cover everything with foil and cook the contents in the oven for 90 mins.
- Serve with the toasted bread.
- Enjoy.

Amount per serving: 18

Timing Information:

Preparation	0 mins
Total Time	1 hr

Nutritional Information:

Calories	77.3
Cholesterol	33.7mg
Sodium	157.1
Carbohydrates	2.4g
Protein	2.2g

* Percent Daily Values are based on a 2,000 calorie diet.

DIJON SCALLION PÂTÉ

Ingredients

- 2 (3 3/4 oz.) cans oil packed sardines, drained
- 2 hard-boiled eggs
- 1/4 C. butter, softened
- 2 tbsps mayonnaise
- 1 1/2 tbsps lemon juice
- 1 tbsp Dijon mustard
- 1/4 celery, finely chopped
- 2 tbsps scallions, finely chopped

Directions

- Add the following to the bowl of a food processor: mustard, sardines, lemon, eggs, mayo, and butter.
- Begin to puree the mix until it is smooth then combine in the scallions and celery by stirring.
- Enjoy.

Amount per serving: 8

Timing Information:

Preparation	20 mins
Total Time	20 mins

Nutritional Information:

Calories	126.5
Cholesterol	99.5mg
Sodium	225.1
Carbohydrates	0.5g
Protein	8.3g

* Percent Daily Values are based on a 2,000 calorie diet.

Irish Apple Mash

Ingredients

- 2 C. water, divided
- 1 tsp brown sugar
- 1 small lemon, halved and juiced, halves reserved
- 1 large apple (such as Honey Crisp), peeled and chopped
- 4 large baking potatoes, peeled and chopped
- 6 C. water
- 3 tbsp butter
- 3 tbsp heavy whipping cream
- 1 tsp salt
- 1 tbsp ground black pepper

Directions

- In a pan, mix together the apple, reserved lemon halves, brown sugar, lemon juice and 2 C. of the water on medium-high heat.
- Boil for about 10-12 minutes and drain well, then transfer into a large bowl.
- Discard the lemon halves and keep the apple slices warm by covering them with foil.

- In a large pan, add the potatoes and 6 C. of the water on medium-high heat.
- Cook everything for 15-20 minutes and drain well.
- Add the potatoes in the bowl with the apple and with a hand blender mash them completely.

Amount per serving (6 total)

Timing Information:

Preparation	15 m
Cooking	25 m
Total Time	40 m

Nutritional Information:

Calories	293 kcal
Fat	8.9 g
Carbohydrates	51g
Protein	5.6 g
Cholesterol	25 mg
Sodium	457 mg

* Percent Daily Values are based on a 2,000 calorie diet.

ALMOND SALSA

Ingredients

- 2/3 C. roasted, salted almonds, finely chopped
- 1 bunch flat-leaf parsley, finely chopped
- 1 clove garlic, minced
- 1 C. olive oil

Directions

- Place your parsley and almonds on a working surface and chop everything evenly.
- Place the mix into a bowl and combine in the garlic.
- Add in the oil and work the mix until a thick sauce forms.
- Enjoy.

Amount per serving (8 total)

Timing Information:

Preparation	15 m
Cooking	15 m
Total Time	30 m

Nutritional Information:

Calories	311 kcal
Fat	33.1 g
Carbohydrates	2.8g
Protein	2.8 g
Cholesterol	0 mg
Sodium	44 mg

* Percent Daily Values are based on a 2,000 calorie diet.

ALMOND JAM

Ingredients

- 1 C. water
- 2 (.25 oz.) envelopes unflavored gelatin powder
- 1 C. water
- 2 C. milk
- 3/4 C. sugar
- 1 1/2 tsps almond extract

Directions

- Get a bowl, combine: water and gelatin.
- Stir the mix for a bit then get another C. of water boiling in a big pot.
- Once the water is boiling set the heat to low and add in the gelatin mix.
- Then combine in the almond extract, milk, and sugar.
- Stir everything until it is well combined and all the gelatin is dissolved then place everything into a dish for storage, in the fridge for 5 hrs.
- Slice the mix into a squares.
- Enjoy.

Amount per serving (6 total)

Timing Information:

Preparation	5 m
Cooking	5 m
Total Time	3 h 10 m

Nutritional Information:

Calories	148 kcal
Fat	1.6 g
Carbohydrates	28.8g
Protein	4.7 g
Cholesterol	7 mg
Sodium	39 mg

* Percent Daily Values are based on a 2,000 calorie diet.

Sriracha Mayo

Ingredients

- 1 C. mayonnaise
- 2 tbsps sriracha hot sauce
- 1 lime, juiced

Directions

- Get a bowl, combine: sriracha and mayo.
- Stir the mix until the sriracha is evenly distributed and the color of the mayo is even.
- Now pour in the lime juice and combine the liquid in.
- Enjoy.

Amount per serving (10 total)

Timing Information:

Preparation	
Cooking	5 m
Total Time	5 m

Nutritional Information:

Calories	160 kcal
Fat	17.5 g
Carbohydrates	1.3g
Protein	< 0.2 g
Cholesterol	< 8 mg
Sodium	252 mg

* Percent Daily Values are based on a 2,000 calorie diet.

Buffalo Salsa

Ingredients

- 3 large ripe tomatoes, diced
- 3 roma (plum) tomatoes, diced
- 4 green onions, finely chopped
- 4 fresh jalapeno peppers, finely diced
- 1 stalk celery, finely diced
- 4 tbsps chopped fresh cilantro
- 1 clove garlic, diced
- 1 tbsp fresh lime juice
- 2 tsps ground black pepper
- salt to taste

Directions

- Get a bowl, combine: salt, tomatoes, pepper, plum tomatoes, lime juice, green onions, garlic, peppers, cilantro, and celery.
- Stir the mix to evenly coat the tomatoes then place a covering of plastic on the bowl and put everything in the fridge for 50 mins.
- Enjoy.

Amount per serving (20 total)

Timing Information:

Preparation	
Cooking	15 m
Total Time	1 h

Nutritional Information:

Calories	10 kcal
Fat	< 0.1 g
Carbohydrates	< 2.2g
Protein	< 0.5 g
Cholesterol	< 0 mg
Sodium	4 mg

* Percent Daily Values are based on a 2,000 calorie diet.

Avocado Salsa

Ingredients

- 1 mango, peeled, seeded and diced
- 1 avocado, peeled, pitted, and diced
- 4 medium tomatoes, diced
- 1 jalapeno pepper, seeded and diced
- 1/2 C. chopped fresh cilantro
- 3 cloves garlic, diced
- 1 tsp salt
- 2 tbsps fresh lime juice
- 1/4 C. chopped red onion
- 3 tbsps olive oil

Directions

- Get a bowl, mix: garlic, mango, cilantro, avocado, and tomatoes.
- Stir the mix then add in your olive oil, salt, red onions, and lime juice.
- Stir your salsa to evenly distribute the liquids. Then place a covering of plastic on the bowl and put everything in the fridge for 40 mins.
- Enjoy.

Amount per serving (6 total)

Timing Information:

Preparation	
Cooking	15 m
Total Time	45 m

Nutritional Information:

Calories	158 kcal
Fat	12 g
Carbohydrates	13.8g
Protein	1.9 g
Cholesterol	0 mg
Sodium	397 mg

* Percent Daily Values are based on a 2,000 calorie diet.

Classical Homemade Guacamole

Ingredients

- 3 avocados, peeled, pitted, and mashed
- 1 lime, juiced
- 1 tsp salt
- 1/2 C. diced onion
- 3 tbsps chopped fresh cilantro
- 2 roma (plum) tomatoes, diced
- 1 tsp diced garlic
- 1 pinch ground cayenne pepper

Directions

- Get a bowl, combine: salt, lime juice, and avocados.
- Stir the mix to evenly coat the avocadoes then combine in: the cayenne, onion, garlic, cilantro, and tomatoes.
- Place a covering of plastic on the bowl and put everything in the fridge for 60 mins.
- Enjoy.

Amount per serving (4 total)

Timing Information:

Preparation	
Cooking	10 m
Total Time	10 m

Nutritional Information:

Calories	262 kcal
Fat	22.2 g
Carbohydrates	18g
Protein	3.7 g
Cholesterol	0 mg
Sodium	596 mg

* Percent Daily Values are based on a 2,000 calorie diet.

Tomato and Avocado Soup

Ingredients

- 2 tbsps vegetable oil
- 1 (1 lb) package frozen pepper and onion veggie mix
- 2 cloves garlic, diced
- 3 tbsps ground cumin
- 1 (28 oz.) can crushed tomatoes
- 3 (4 oz.) cans chopped green chili peppers, drained
- 4 (14 oz.) cans vegetable broth
- salt and pepper to taste
- 1 (11 oz.) can whole kernel corn
- 12 oz. tortilla chips
- 1 C. shredded Cheddar cheese
- 1 avocado, peeled, pitted and diced

Directions

- Stir fry your onions and peppers for 2 mins in hot oil then add in the cumin and garlic. Continue frying the mix for 4 more mins until the veggies are soft.
- Now combine in the chili peppers and tomatoes.
- Stir the mix again and let the pepper cook for 30 secs before adding in some pepper, salt, and the broth.

- Now get everything boiling, set the heat to low, and let the mix gently simmer for 35 mins.
- Add in the corn to the mix and let the veggies cook for 7 mins.
- When serving the soup top each individual serving with some tortilla chips, avocado, and cheese.
- Enjoy.

Amount per serving (12 total)

Timing Information:

Preparation	15 m
Cooking	40 m
Total Time	55 m

Nutritional Information:

Calories	315 kcal
Fat	16.2 g
Carbohydrates	37.2g
Protein	8.7 g
Cholesterol	12 mg
Sodium	1152 mg

* Percent Daily Values are based on a 2,000 calorie diet.

CILANTRO AND GARBANZO SOUP

Ingredients

- 1 green bell pepper
- 1 medium tomato
- 1 yellow onion
- 1 large carrot
- 1 baking potato
- 1 (15 oz.) can garbanzo beans, drained
- 2 eggs
- 3 tbsps olive oil
- 1 tsp salt
- 1/2 tsp ground black pepper
- 1/2 tsp hot pepper sauce
- 1/2 tsp ground turmeric
- 1 tbsp chopped fresh cilantro
- 1 cube vegetable bouillon
- 8 C. water

Directions

- Cook sliced vegetables in hot oil along with salt, hot sauce and pepper for three minutes before stirring in water, turmeric, garbanzo beans, coriander and bouillon cube, and bringing all this to boil.
- Now add eggs before turning down the heat to low and cooking for thirty minutes.

- Peel the egg, slice it and put it back into the pan before cooking it on low for 20 minutes.
- Serve this over couscous.

Serving: 3

Timing Information:

Preparation	Cooking	Total Time
15 mins	1 hr	1 hr 15 mins

Nutritional Information:

Calories	377 kcal
Fat	18.3 g
Cholesterol	124 mg
Sodium	1152 mg
Carbohydrates	43.8 g
Fiber	8.4 g
Protein	11.7 g

* Percent Daily Values are based on a 2,000 calorie diet.

SUNDAY SOUP

Ingredients

- 2 tbsps olive oil
- 2 large onions, cubed
- 1 tsp minced garlic
- 3 carrots, minced
- 2 stalks celery, minced
- 3 1/2 C. mashed tomatoes
- 1 1/2 C. lentils - soaked, rinsed and drained
- 1/2 tsp salt
- 1/2 tsp ground black pepper
- 3/4 C. white wine
- 2 bay leaves
- 7 C. chicken stock
- 1 sprig fresh parsley, chopped
- 1/2 tsp paprika
- 1/2 C. grated Parmesan cheese

Directions

- Cook onions in hot oil for a few minutes and then add garlic, paprika, celery and carrots before cooking all this for 10 more minutes.
- Now stir in tomatoes, bay leaves, chicken stock, lentils, wine, salt, and pepper before bringing everything to boil and cooking on low heat for one hour.
- Sprinkle some parsley and parmesan before serving.

Serving: 8

Timing Information:

Preparation	Cooking	Total Time
15 mins	1 hr 15 mins	1 hr 30 mins

Nutritional Information:

Calories	255 kcal
Fat	6 g
Cholesterol	9 mg
Sodium	1099 mg
Carbohydrates	33.3 g
Fiber	13.7 g
Protein	13.7 g

* Percent Daily Values are based on a 2,000 calorie diet.

CANNELLINI AND TOMATO SOUP

Ingredients

- 1 tbsp olive oil
- 2 lbs bulk Italian sausage
- 2 (32 oz.) cartons chicken broth
- 2 (15 oz.) cans cannellini beans, rinsed and drained
- 1 head escarole, chopped
- 1 (15 oz.) can tomato sauce

Directions

- Cook sausage in hot olive oil for 10 minutes before adding chicken broth, beans, escarole, and tomato sauce into the pan.
- Cook on low heat for 20 minutes.
- Serve.

Serving: 14

Timing Information:

Preparation	Cooking	Total Time
10 mins	20 mins	30 mins

Nutritional Information:

Calories	303 kcal
Fat	19.4 g
Cholesterol	40 mg
Sodium	1688 mg
Carbohydrates	15 g
Fiber	4.3 g
Protein	16.4 g

* Percent Daily Values are based on a 2,000 calorie diet.

THANKS FOR READING! JOIN THE CLUB AND KEEP ON COOKING WITH 6 MORE COOKBOOKS....

http://bit.ly/1TdrStv

 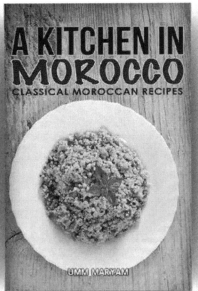 

To grab the box sets simply follow the link mentioned above, or tap one of book covers.

This will take you to a page where you can simply enter your email address and a PDF version of the box sets will be emailed to you.

Hope you are ready for some serious cooking!

http://bit.ly/1TdrStv

Come On...
Let's Be Friends :)

We adore our readers and love connecting with them socially.

Like BookSumo on Facebook and let's get social!

Facebook

And also check out the BookSumo Cooking Blog.

Food Lover Blog

Made in the USA
Lexington, KY
19 July 2017